Sir Edwin Lutyens

An illustrated life of Sir Edwin Lutyens
(1869–1944)

Michael Barker

A Shire book

Sir Edwin Lutyens

For Eliza and Sam

Cover: *Portrait of Sir Edwin Lutyens, by Meredith Frampton, 1933.*

British Library Cataloguing in Publication Data: Barker, Michael. Sir Edwin Lutyens: an illustrated life of Sir Edwin Lutyens, 1869-1944. – (Lifelines; 43). 1. Lutyens, Edwin Landseer, Sir, 1869-1944. 2. Architects – Great Britain – Biography. I. Title. 720.9'2. ISBN 0 7478 0582 2.

ACKNOWLEDGEMENTS
The portrait on the front cover is reproduced by courtesy of The Art Workers' Guild. The photograph of the author on the back cover is by Graham Miller. Other illustrations are acknowledged as follows: the French Government Tourist Office, Piccadilly, pages 36 (top), 37 (bottom); Veronica Franklin Gould, page 45; Cadbury Lamb, pages 5, 18 (top), 20, 23, 24, 25, 29, 32 (bottom), 34, 37, 39 (top); Liverpool Museums, page 42; Candia Lutyens, pages 4, 14, 32 (top), 44 (top), 46; Christopher Page, page 47; the Viscount Ridley, pages 3, 13, 35, 36 (bottom). All other illustrations are by the author.
    The author is grateful for the invaluable help of Margaret Richardson, the Viscount Ridley, Candia Lutyens, Peyton Skipwith and the Commonwealth War Graves Commission, and the support of the Lutyens Trust.

Published in 2005 by Shire Publications Ltd, Cromwell House, Church Street, Princes Risborough, Buckinghamshire HP27 9AA, UK. Website: www.shirebooks.co.uk Copyright © 2005 by Michael Barker. First published 2005. Number 43 in the Lifelines series. ISBN 0 7478 0582 2.

Printed in Malta by Gutenberg Press Limited, Gudja Road, Tarxien PLA 19, Malta.

Contents

Lutyens at Mansfield Street with his grandson Matthew Ridley after receiving the KCIE in 1930.

Lutyens at the peak of his career.

The humane face of genius

Edwin Lutyens was England's greatest and most prolific architect since Christopher Wren. His career lasted more than half a century, from the reign of Queen Victoria, whose empire spanned the globe, until the Second World War. With little formal education or architectural training, Lutyens precociously set up as an architect on his own account at the age of nineteen. In the early days, rooted in the Arts and Crafts movement, he built the first of his many picturesque country houses, mainly in Surrey, where he spent much of his childhood. His work, while romantic in inspiration, became classical in discipline, yet complex and often abstract in design, and was always executed with excellent craftsmanship, using fine materials.

Lutyens dominated the Edwardian era as the architect of new country houses for new fortunes. His Viceroy's House at New Delhi, larger than Versailles, is perhaps the most magnificent palace of modern times. After the First World War, in the wake of his Cenotaph in Whitehall whose symbolism captured the public imagination, he created

many war memorials, monuments and military cemeteries, beautifully landscaped and of utmost originality, which movingly paid due tribute to the Fallen. There were fewer country houses after 1918 but commissions came for palatial banks, notably Midland Bank in the City of London, at the time the largest in the world, and other important commercial premises such

The wrought-iron screen of the former Viceroy's House, New Delhi (now the Presidential Palace). This was one of Lutyens's greatest works. Larger than the Palace of Versailles, it was a major preoccupation of his career from 1911 until the 1930s.

5

The Cenotaph, Whitehall. As the national memorial to the Fallen of the British Empire in the First World War and the scene of remembrance every year on the anniversary of the Armistice, it is the best known and most widely revered of Lutyens's monuments.

as Britannic House and Reuters. What would have been his greatest work, larger than St Peter's Basilica in Rome – the Roman Catholic Liverpool Cathedral – was never achieved; only its crypt was built.

Given his small office and the exigencies of travel, Lutyens's output of more than six hundred commissions in England, Wales, Scotland, Ireland, France, Belgium, Germany, Spain, Italy, Hungary, South Africa, India and the United States is astonishing. All were meticulously designed by him; assistants merely did the donkey-work. His genius lay in his unerring sense of proportion in a variety of idioms, often introducing a note of gaiety, and his ability to create works of charm but also great monuments of grave character. In contrast, Lutyens was bad at business and paid scant attention to finances, which gave him money worries throughout his life. His family life was also fraught; his aristocratic wife, Lady Emily Lytton, gave him little support at home, was often away and pursued the creed of Theosophy with an obsession for its guru, Jiddu Krishnamurti. While the couple's enormous correspondence displays much mutual affection, after giving Lutyens five children Lady Emily denied him his marital rights. She became a feminist, a vegetarian and a socialist, in contrast to her husband, who held the conventional views of his generation.

Ostensibly Lutyens was charming and humorous – though some found his endless puns tiresome – but underneath he was quite ruthless and ambitious; he was a perfectionist, existing in single-minded pursuit of his architectural ideals. Lutyens was highly influential in the revival of modern classicism. He was knighted in 1918, was President of the Royal Academy 1938–44, and was the first architect to be awarded, in 1942, the Order of Merit.

Early days

In 1869, in a tall Italianate terraced house at 16 Onslow Square in South Kensington, Mary Lutyens gave birth on 29th March to her eleventh child, christened Edwin Landseer in the new church of St Paul nearby – a focal point of the devout Mary's life. There were to be thirteen children in all (and one stillborn), ten sons and three daughters. Mary's husband, Captain Charles Lutyens, was an army officer turned hunting man and animal painter. Charles had inherited sufficient means to maintain a large family in some comfort without having to work particularly hard an artist. Onslow Square was a respectable address in the fairly recent expansion of London west of Knightsbridge, with the development of stucco terraces in full swing. The Albert Memorial, the Albert Hall and the museums were still under construction. The

16 Onslow Square, the family home in South Kensington, was Lutyens's birthplace in 1869.

Lutyens family's neighbours included William Thackeray, Baron Marochetti (Queen Victoria's favourite sculptor) and William Railton, designer of Nelson's Column in Trafalgar Square, the four lions at the foot of which were by Edwin Landseer, patron and teacher of Charles, who paid him the compliment of naming his new son after the great man, the most famous painter of the day. Mary, however, refused to allow him to be her son's godfather, given his lack of religion and his immoral ways as the lover of the Duchess of Bedford and the father of illegitimate children.

Charles Lutyens met and married Mary Gallwey in Canada in 1852. This nineteen-year-old dark-haired Irish beauty, daughter of a general, was staying with her brother, a major in the Royal Engineers, while Charles was serving with the Lancashire Fusiliers. Charles was the fourth generation of his family to live in England, his great-grandfather, Bartold Lütkens, a merchant from Hamburg (probably of Dutch origin), having arrived in 1739. Returning to England, the couple, both orphans, settled in Winchester, Hampshire. When the Crimean War broke out in 1854, Charles's regiment was sent abroad but detained in Malta. By the time he reached the Crimea, the war was over. Leaving the army in 1857, thus just avoiding being sent to quell the Indian Mutiny, Charles devoted himself to his painting and his family, based in London until 1876, when he rented a house in the attractive Surrey village of Thursley.

The young Edwin – who hated the name and preferred to be called Ned – was a rather sickly child, suffering from regular bouts of rheumatic fever, its only cure then being complete rest. Inevitably this meant close contact with his adored mother (from whom he inherited dark, curly hair and big blue eyes) and it gave him plenty of time to think and to teach himself the value of using his eyes. He later claimed that his adult success derived from this opportunity. The new house at Thursley, now readily accessible by train, became Ned's preferred base. Although called The Cottage, it was a stuccoed Regency sash-windowed house with six bedrooms and a walled garden that stood out from the predominantly tile-hung and half-timbered vernacular of the area – the painting field of the picturesque of Birket Foster and Helen Allingham.

Following lessons at home with his sisters and a two-year spell at a boarding school in Wimbledon, Ned was deemed too delicate for public school – a decision taken partly for financial reasons, Charles's fortune having dwindled. As an adult, Ned bitterly regretted not having gone to a decent public school like his peers. Between the ages of thirteen and fifteen Ned, fascinated by nature and buildings, roamed west Surrey with a framed pane of glass on which he sketched with sharpened pieces of soap. He spent many hours in the village carpenter's shop or in a local builder's yard. Thanks to the encouragement of a local resident, the artist Randolph Caldecott, just before his sixteenth birthday Ned enrolled at the South Kensington School of Art (later the Royal College of Art), a short walk from Onslow Square.

Most of his time was spent following the national architecture course, which focused on the classical orders, Gothic architecture and construction – including the use of iron, ornament in building and architectural design. The teaching seems to have been mediocre and Ned did not complete the course but entered as an articled pupil in late 1887 the office of Ernest George, a busy and successful architectural practice working for the Grosvenor Estate in Mayfair, the Cadogan Estate in Chelsea, and building many country houses. Herbert Baker, then a senior assistant, who became a friend and much later a rival of Ned's, noted that he showed little application to his work but seemed to absorb by observation what he felt to be worthwhile. Ned, no great admirer of his boss – his hero was Norman Shaw – stayed just a year and a half but his drawing had improved and he had learnt more than he cared to admit. Despite his professed scorn of sketching, Ned went on tour in France as a student and produced both sketches and measured drawings of numerous buildings in Normandy, which had a certain influence on his work later, as did such buildings as Stokesay Castle and Wenlock Priory, visited on a walking tour in Shropshire and the Welsh borders with Herbert Baker.

1889 was a momentous year. Aged nineteen, with little formal education, minimal training as an architect and no professional experience, Ned boldly set himself up as an architect, at first in Onslow Square, but later he put up his brass plate at 6 Gray's Inn Square, armed with a £100 legacy, an elderly assistant and his first important commission, Crooksbury, for businessman Arthur (later Sir Arthur) Chapman. This was instigated by Barbara Webb, married to a dull Surrey squire but a clever and cultured woman who responded very sympathetically to Ned, taking him under her wing and introducing him in London society, to new clients and to the woman who became his wife. He loved Barbara until her early death from cancer in 1897.

Ned cut his teeth with a gardener's cottage for Harry Mangles, the rhododendron grower, in Thursley and additions to a cottage opposite his parents' house – both influenced by Ernest George. But Crooksbury, for Arthur Chapman, who knew the Lutyens family, was Ned's first significant building. Understandably it made him nervous, and a smoking chimney gave him a typical building problem to solve. While owing a debt to George and Norman Shaw, Crooksbury, praised by the critic Ian Nairn, gave a hint of a fresh English style – found predominantly in Surrey – which for several years until 1900 led the world in domestic architecture. In May, Ned was introduced by Harry Mangles to another woman who was to be of utmost importance in his life. Gertrude Jekyll (rhyming with 'treacle' not 'heckle'), then forty-five, was a plain, dumpy, myopic and rather formidable spinster but worldly and well connected in upper-class circles and in the arts: Ruskin and Whistler were among her friends. Gertrude was first a talented artist, embroiderer and craftswoman but it was as a horticulturist and plantswoman that her vision revolutionised garden design.

Evidently Gertrude Jekyll perceived something in this shy young man at their meeting since she invited him to visit her the following week. And so began a close friendship and fruitful collaboration that lasted until Gertrude's death in 1932 – she Ned's fairy godmother and mentor; he, at least initially, the willing pupil of 'Bumps', as he called her. They enjoyed exploring rural Surrey together in her erratically driven pony cart, looking at old buildings and gardens with a lively

Gertrude Jekyll. A drawing by Lutyens of his beloved mentor, made about 1896.

Munstead Wood, Surrey, built in the local Bargate stone for a delighted Gertrude Jekyll, was much admired by the architect Robert Lorimer and considerably enhanced the young Lutyens's reputation in Arts and Crafts circles.

exchange of views. Through Gertrude and her younger brother Herbert, Ned made many new friends and, important for his career, a good number of them became, or led to, new clients. For Adeline, newly the widow of the tenth Duke of Bedford, Gertrude and Ned designed a formal garden at Woodside, near Chenies, in Buckinghamshire. Otherwise, Ned's jobs for the next few years were almost entirely in Surrey. Gertrude, with her widowed mother, lived at Munstead House, near Godalming, built by Gertrude's father in the 1870s. When her brother Herbert (later Sir Herbert Jekyll) inherited the house, Gertrude needed a home of her own. She had already planned and partly planted a garden at Munstead and Ned had designed a picturesque cottage for her there in 1894 called The Hut, but Gertrude wanted a dream house. The result was Munstead Wood, built near The Hut in 1896–7. It was very much a collaboration; she knew exactly what she wanted in its planning to serve her needs but Ned created, with its inventive free Tudor style, finely crafted, a notable work of Arts and Crafts architecture. For Her Royal Highness Princess Louise, Marchioness of Lorne and later Duchess of Argyll, introduced by Gertrude, Ned carried out large extensions in 1896–7 to the Ferry Inn, Rosneath, Dunbartonshire, experimenting with details verging on the Art Nouveau style. He also executed alterations at her house at Inveraray for this capricious daughter of Queen Victoria and talented sculptress.

Marriage and early fame

In the early summer of 1896 another significant woman came into Ned's life, espied across a Kensington drawing-room when Barbara Webb took him to a musical soirée at Jacques Blumenthal's house at 43 Hyde Park Gate. The focus of his attention was Lady Emily Lytton, quite tall with pale golden hair though not actually very pretty. She was looking rather cross. Emily had recently had an unfortunate infatuation with Wilfred Scawen Blunt, married but a notorious womaniser, a friend of her late father, the statesman and poet Robert, first Earl of Lytton, Viceroy of India and Ambassador in Paris, who died in 1891. Emily was brought up at Knebworth in Hertfordshire, a romantic sham castle encasing an Elizabethan house, created by her grandfather, the writer Bulwer Lytton. Ned insisted on being introduced.

While they met from time to time at dances that summer it was not until September, when Emily stayed with Barbara Webb at Milford, that the besotted Ned made any sort of progress. He took Emily to meet Gertrude Jekyll at The Hut, which Emily enjoyed, and there was an obvious *frisson* when he took her on a moonlit jaunt to see one of his current projects. But, unkindly, aware that he was smitten, she played with his affections, having some yearning for Gerald Duckworth (spending that summer at his stepfather's house at Hindhead with his step-sisters – the future Virginia Woolf and Vanessa Bell). Duckworth, later a respected publisher, did not respond, however, to this young woman's desire to escape the parental yoke by marriage.

Despite the qualms of both Barbara Webb and Gertrude Jekyll about the wisdom of such a match – of an aristocrat with an architect of little means – Ned persevered with his courtship. Emily, already feeling on the shelf at twenty-two, became intrigued by his possibilities as a genius and began to see him as someone who could provide a focus to her rather unfulfilled life. Ned designed an enchanting casket to contain various treasures and plans of 'a little white house' – to be their ideal home in the country – never realised; they always lived in London.

But a major obstacle to their union was Emily's mother, Edith, Countess of Lytton, recently widowed and financially insecure owing to her husband's latter improvidence. Her concern was Ned's financial expectations – let alone his unsuitability, being middle class and without capital. Eventually, Ned having mortgaged his future income with a costly insurance policy, Edith relented and in January 1897 the terrified Ned was summoned to Hertfordshire – to The Danes, since the family seat of Knebworth was let. And so the match was finally approved, the wedding taking place at

Knebworth in August. The honeymoon was spent in Surrey and then by the seaside in Holland. The sexually inexperienced Ned, deeply in love with his bride and proudly a virgin, proved to be an inadequate lover; the honeymoon was not a success and the root cause of its disappointment was to colour the rest of their life together.

They returned to a borrowed house in Kensington at 24 Addison Road in which they stayed until December. The marital home chosen by Ned was 29 Bloomsbury Square, formerly the office of Ned's hero Norman Shaw. Their move just before Christmas was inauspicious: the premium was more than he could easily afford, Emily was pregnant, and the big Georgian house was bare of furniture and unheated, but it was to be their home until 1912 and Ned's office occupied the ground floor until 1910. Eschewing the untidy bohemian chaos of his parents' house, Ned adopted a rather modern, uncluttered interior, decorated with black walls in the drawing-room, with white ceilings and woodwork, green and white drag-painted floors and yellow curtains; the dining-room had Venetian red walls. Their first-born, Barbara, arrived in August 1898, followed by Robert in 1901. Emily was not keen on living in London and was often in the country staying with her mother or with friends or relations. As Ned was also often away, endlessly on trains with his work spread far and wide, it is little wonder that their correspondence during their entire, uneasy married life was so voluminous.

Professionally, 1897 was the *annus mirabilis* of Lutyens's early career.

A drawing of Lutyens by Edmund Dulac on a train in 1922, inscribed 'between Dover and London'.

There were so many (at least twenty-five) projects that year that it is difficult to comprehend how he coped given that he was not a sharp businessman nor had he an army of assistants to take the strain. Mrs Chance, née Julia Strachey, a sculptor, married to William Chance (later knighted), a successful QC and radical but the scion of a family of rich glass manufacturers, spotted Munstead Wood. The Chances had a building site nearby and a projected house by Halsey Ricardo with which they were disappointed. Gertrude, mindful of Ned's need for a substantial commission to support his new bride, talked the Chances into engaging him. The result, Orchards, was the finest of his early works, its garden designed with Gertrude. Its layout has a rather French feel with its approach bound by buttressed outbuildings leading to an archway into a large courtyard.

On a ridge with splendid views at Elstead, Surrey, Ned built Fulbrook, an expensive house designed for Gerard Streatfield – a commission encouraged by Barbara Webb. Streatfield's wife's father, Richard Combe, had commissioned Norman Shaw twenty years earlier to build Pierrepont at Frensham. Fulbrook was described by Ned's biographer Christopher Hussey in 1950 as the worst house he ever made but it was much admired by later critics – though many noted the oddity of the classical detail of the staircase within a vernacular house. Ned, now aged twenty-seven, was experimenting in design, introducing sophistication but also some eccentricity to his Arts and Crafts *oeuvre*, which encompassed much diversity, pre-dating the avant-garde of C. R. Mackintosh in

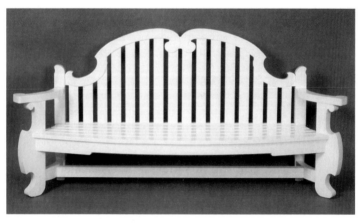

A garden bench that appears to have been designed c.1897 for Fulbrook in Surrey, one of his early major country houses.

14

Le Bois des Moutiers, near Dieppe, Normandy. The first of his works in France, this house is in the Arts and Crafts style but with Free Style elements and with gardens designed in collaboration with Gertrude Jekyll. It is still in the hands of the Mallet family, for whom it was built in 1898.

Scotland (which Ned espied in Glasgow in 1897). For Cyril Flower, made Lord Battersea by Gladstone, Ned created a curious house out of a pair of villas: The Pleasaunce at Overstrand on the bracing Norfolk coast, not much liked by Lady Battersea, née Constance de Rothschild. Its construction apparently went on for some years. In the same village Ned built in 1898 his only Nonconformist chapel – also for Lord Battersea – and in the following year the inventive Overstrand Hall for Charles Mills, second Baron Hillingdon, a partner in Glynn Mills, the banking firm.

As the century and the reign of Queen Victoria drew to a close, Ned was on the brink of entering a spectacular rise in his career. The domesticity of rural west Surrey receded for a more national, even international, scene. But, still in Surrey, for the daughter of Sir Edgar Horne, a local Member of Parliament and Chairman of the Prudential, Ned designed Tigbourne Court at Witley in 1899, one of his most elegant and distinctive houses, built in Bargate stone, standing right on the main road for all to see. It became something of a showcase for his talent.

A series of walled gardens planted by Gertrude Jekyll in front of Le Bois des Moutiers. This design may have been inspired by the eighteenth-century garden of Canon in Lower Normandy. The pergola beyond featured in many of Lutyens's garden designs.

Through Herbert Jekyll, who was on the committee for the 1900 Paris Exhibition, Ned was given the job of building the British Pavilion – a pastiche of 'an Elizabethan house'. He reported that it gave him 'no scope for originality in design', but it was awarded a Grand Prix and the resulting prestige was most welcome, leading to the commission from Guillaume Mallet, a Protestant banker, to rebuild Le Bois des Moutiers, his country house at Varengeville in Normandy (still in the hands of the family), the first of several commissions from the Mallets. The family became lifelong friends of Ned and Emily, with dire consequences for their marital life. In bosky surroundings, on high ground overlooking the English Channel, Le Bois des Moutiers is contemporary with Orchards but, far from Surrey, Ned introduced elements close to the Art Nouveau style for the first time, while still employing English Arts and Crafts design. Its interior, retaining much of the original house, is relatively conventional but the excitement comes from climbing the stairs to enter the balcony of the music-room: through a tall faceted window, there is a sudden dramatic plunging view down to the sea. The lovely gardens were designed with Gertrude: close to the front of the house is a series of formal walled courtyards but the extensive park is planted with rare species of trees and shrubs, notably rhododendrons and azaleas.

The Edwardian years

Lady Lytton, having come to terms with the fact that her daughter had married an architect and having actually become quite fond of Ned, looked to him for a dower house at Knebworth for her and Constance, her unmarried daughter, which was to be paid for by her son Victor, the second Earl. Its design evolved in 1900 and it was built the following year. At first sight Homewood seems to be a simple vernacular house with weatherboarded triple gables, but a closer examination reveals a rather clever design of some complexity, incorporating Mannerist detail. The house was not very well constructed by Knebworth's estate builders, with corners cut since the Lyttons were short of funds, and with a few infelicities – the drawing-room was too dark, thought Emily – but Ned's daughter Mary had fond memories of it having no electricity but 'the cosy smell of oil lamps'. Lady Lytton never used the bathroom; until her death aged ninety-five in 1936 she preferred a tin tub in front of the fire.

In 1899 Ned met a man who became a lifelong friend, a substantial patron and a generous champion of his achievements. Edward Hudson, a printer's son, founded his magazine *Country Life* in 1897 as a vehicle for his interests. Gertrude contributed gardening notes anonymously.

The first of Ned's houses to appear in *Country Life* was Orchards, in 1900. Hudson, a bachelor, now became a client. The first house designed for him by Ned was Deanery Garden at Sonning, Berkshire, in 1901. A romantic red-brick house built in an ancient walled orchard, it was integrated into the village in a way that Ned was to do quite often – creating grand houses right on the street. By complete contrast, Hudson acquired in 1902 the ruins of Lindisfarne Castle, a Tudor fort on Holy Island off the Northumberland coast, which

3 Southampton Street, Covent Garden. The clock was designed by Lutyens in 1904 for the printers George Newnes.

Lindisfarne Castle, Northumberland, which Lutyens converted into a country residence for Edward Hudson.

42 Kingsway was built in 1906 in a newly created London street as the offices of 'The Garden', a magazine founded by Edward Hudson and the cantankerous William Robinson, promoter of naturalistic gardening.

Langley End in Hertfordshire, one of Lutyens's picturesque small houses of 1914, was praised by 'Country Life' writer Lawrence Weaver in his book 'Small Country Houses of Today'.

he wanted Ned to make habitable as a holiday house. It was completed in 1906. Ned and Gertrude went to stay there and Gertrude later laid out a small walled garden. As a successful publishing venture, *Country Life* needed offices. Ned's first building in London, built in 1904 in Covent Garden, was his first public building and also his first essay in London in a neo-William and Mary style: this was his adaptation of Wren's ranges at Hampton Court Palace, which he called 'Wrenaissance'. The enterprise represented his move towards what he called the 'High Game' of Palladio and Wren – to be fully realised in 1906 at 42 Kingsway, offices for *The Garden*, a magazine created by the horticulturist William Robinson.

The expansive Edwardian era produced new fortunes, the usual way to show them off being to have a grand house and become a country gentleman. Those with old money mostly had their ancestral estates and were generally little interested in new architecture. As opposed to the raffish circle of Edward VII, which was not Ned's world, his patrons made or inherited their money from trade, industry or the law; their fortunes were not huge but were large enough for them to commission a decent house from the architect whose name was becoming known from the pages of *Country Life* or through family connections. Ned's

Grey Walls, Gullane, East Lothian, commissioned by the Honourable Alfred Lyttelton, a member of the literary coterie the 'Souls' and a keen golfer, to be close to the Muirfield links. Grey Walls was built in a vernacular Georgian style by Lutyens from 1902 but sold to the rich collector William James, a friend of Edward VII, for whom Lutyens added lodges in 1909.

success caused a certain jealousy in the profession, fellow architects putting it down to his having made a 'society marriage'. One client who was not of the new rich was the well-born Honourable Alfred Lyttelton, sportsman and lawyer, later a Member of Parliament and member of the 'Souls', a high-minded coterie of intellectuals. For this keen golfer (a new craze for the Edwardians) Ned built Grey Walls, by the Muirfield Links at Gullane in East Lothian, Scotland. Constructed of rubble stone with casement windows under a pantiled roof, though large for a holiday home, it mixes this rustic detail with a classical interior and the front door has an elaborate broken-pedimented Georgian door-case.

The flow of Ned's most pleasing houses continued in the early years of the new century with Marsh Court on the River Test in Hampshire, designed in 1901 for Herbert Johnson, another sportsman, who had made a fortune in the City as a stock-jobber. It was the largest and among the last of his houses in a free Tudor style (though a more severe, stripped Tudor style did appear later) that used classical detail within. Marsh Court was notable for being built of hard chalk, which gave it a gleaming white appearance reminiscent of buildings in the Loire valley. Its long horizontal windows on the front elevation almost prefigure the modernism of Le Corbusier. Johnson became a lifelong friend and Ned added a ballroom for him in 1924–6. In Sussex, Little Thakeham of 1902–4, which Ned called 'the best of the bunch' (meaning of his houses at the time), is one of Ned's most serene works. Tom Blackburn, a talented amateur gardener, having inherited a family fortune, retired as a schoolmaster and bought 26 acres (10.5 hectares) near the South Downs. Ned took over from an architect who had been sacked by Blackburn – which caused a bit of a scandal, but the Royal Institute of British Architects exonerated him. This symmetrically gabled Tudor house of local stone with leaded-light windows contains a surprising great hall, lit by a tall Tudor oriel window but juxtaposed with a classical screen and wrought-iron balconies.

Ned's only major work in the Cotswolds was Abbotswood, near Stow-on-the-Wold, rebuilding a dreary Victorian house on a wonderful site. Mark and Polly Fenwick, an attractive and well-off couple in their forties with four daughters, became favourite clients. Ned wanted to pull down the existing house but in the event, from 1902, he settled for a substantial remodelling, producing a quirky, inventive design with an enormous gable on the entrance front that reached almost to the ground. The south front, overlooking a broad terrace with a reflecting pool, has narrow twin gables flanking a classical quoined projecting central bay – 'period' detail but unmistakably 'Lutyens'. Mark Fenwick, a passionate gardener, created with Ned new landscaping and planting that are famous to this day.

One of Ned's strangest houses, Papillon Hall in Leicestershire of 1903, was ill-fated. Captain Frank Belleville, a hunting man whose money came from mustard, wanted to enlarge an old house built by the Papillon family to make a hunting box in fashionable country. In the old house was a cupboard containing a pair of eighteenth-century brocade women's shoes; the title deeds stated that they would bring bad fortune if removed. When the shoes were sent away for safe keeping, there were indeed unhappy consequences: slow progress with the project, accidents on site including a worker killed, a motoring accident in which Belleville fractured his skull and his chauffeur died, the non-return from missions of American airmen who occupied the house during the war and, finally, the demolition of the house in 1950 – the only major work of Ned's to suffer this fate.

Although in 1903 Ned failed to secure the job of building a big house on the Hudson River, New York, for the American multimillionaire railwayman E. H. Harriman, he did build Monkton House in Sussex for William James, another rich American (who also made his fortune from railways), who bought the West Dean Estate and Grey Walls from Alfred Lyttelton. Monkton, a modest retreat up in the beechwoods on the estate, was intended for James's wife (a natural daughter of Edward VII). In Northamptonshire, for the Honourable Ivor Guest, later Lord Wimborne, Ned so transformed the historic Catesby family house, Ashby St Ledgers, that it was almost more Lutyens-Tudor than the original manor. Guest, with an American fortune and the family business, Guest, Keen & Nettlefold, returned from the Second Boer War to become a Member of Parliament and married Alice Grosvenor. Ashby was to be their country home, in which they lived in lavish style. Ned had an eye on the Blenheim connection as Ivor's mother was the sister of the Duke of Marlborough and Winston Churchill was a cousin. Ned also built a house in the village for the land agent and a picturesque row of thatched cottages.

An advertisement in *The Field* in 1904 for an island up for sale in the Irish Sea, 3 miles (4.8 km) off the coast of County Dublin, caught the eye of the Honourable Cecil Baring, later Lord Revelstoke, of the banking family, then repairing their fortunes after their bank's huge crash in 1890. Ned was summoned to view their £5250 purchase of Lambay Island with its derelict Tudor fort, which he rebuilt and considerably extended. The Barings were the family that Ned and Emily Lutyens and their children knew best and Cecil helped Ned with introductions to new clients and, importantly, with loans. Ever since the Lytton family's condition of his marriage to Emily that he take out an expensive insurance policy to underpin his practice, Ned was endlessly worried about his finances – a regular feature of his correspondence.

At Thursley, Ned's mother, Mary Lutyens, had lain slowly dying for most of the year following a stroke; her end came in September 1906. Ned was cruising in the Baltic at the time with Herbert and Aggie Jekyll on the luxury yacht of Mary Dodge, a rich American. He was at first reluctant to leave his mother but was feeling overworked

Hestercombe, Cheddon Fitzpaine, Somerset. To embellish an ugly Victorian country house, Lutyens created for the Honourable E. W. Portman from 1904, in collaboration with Gertrude Jekyll, an ingeniously landscaped garden with water features and, as a set piece, a great orangery in an inventive English Baroque style called by Lutyens 'The High Game'.

and badly needed a break. The cruise did allow him to rest, but he missed his mother's funeral. His grief drew him closer to Emily for a while. Ned designed a simple white cross for his mother's grave in Thursley churchyard. He inherited her gold ring, which from then on he wore on the little finger of his left hand. In the same year his fourth child, Elizabeth, was born and on a single day in May four clients signed contracts for important houses.

At Hestercombe, Somerset, the Honourable Edward Portman's mansion built in 1875, Ned laid out the gardens, planted by Gertrude, with an ingenious use of levels and water features and built an orangery in a powerful Vanbrughian style. One of Ned's new clients of 1906 was a rich Yorkshire wool merchant, John Thomas Hemingway, whose villa, Heathcote at Ilkley, West Yorkshire, was the culmination of Ned's long-gestating concept of building in an inventive classical style. The result was astonishing: an elaborate mixture of themes drawn from Sanmicheli and Palladio distilled into something uniquely Lutyens; it came as a shock to many after all the romantic houses for which he

The steps and gate at Hestercombe, Somerset.

was known. Heathcote marked Ned's profound shift to the classical, though Barton St Mary at Forest Row, Sussex, of the same date is in his earlier Free Tudor style and New Place, Shedfield, Hampshire, is a severe, unlovely neo-Jacobean dark-red-brick mansion for Mrs Franklyn incorporating actual Jacobean interiors from a house in Bristol. Ned rightly regarded New Place as a flop.

Almost as costly as Heathcote (£17,500) was Nashdom at Taplow, Buckinghamshire, for Princess Alexis Dolgorouki, born Fanny Wilson, who was talked up to £15,000 from her initial budget of £6,000 for it. Intended for weekend parties, this essay in the neo-Georgian style, with tall, quite bare white-painted elevations and apple-green shutters, has an urban feel; it would have looked perfectly at home on a site in London.

Ned's ambition for the 'High Game' now looked promising. He was one of eight architects invited to enter the competition for a new headquarters on the Thames for the London County Council. His Baroque design, inspired by Greenwich, was a strong favourite but did not succeed, to Ned's great dismay after nine months' work and high hopes. The winner, announced in January 1908, was the little-known Ralph

Knott, a pupil of Aston Webb, one of the assessors. There may have been some favouritism in the decision, but Knott's design was perhaps more in tune with Edwardian fashion.

Ned's disappointment was lessened by commissions for two big houses: huge extensions in keeping with a Queen Anne nucleus at Temple Dinsley in Hertfordshire for Bertie Fenwick, and the rebuilding of Great Maytham in Kent for the Liberal politician Jack Tennant. The Kent house, the setting for the famous children's story *The Secret Garden*, is handsome enough – very tall, in a somewhat over-blown Edwardian neo-Georgian style, but beautifully detailed in blue-grey brick with red-brick dressings, Ned's favourite material at the time – but the mellow-brick Temple Dinsley, regarded as a major work by Christopher Hussey, is the prettier of the two.

Ned had long wanted to build a church and his chance came with the proposed Hampstead Garden Suburb, the fruition of a desire by the formidable Dame Henrietta Barnett, the avid social reformer, to

Great Maytham, Rolvenden, Kent, was a grand Edwardian neo-Georgian country house built by Lutyens in 1907–9 for the Liberal politician Jack Tennant in mellow contrasting brickwork, a favourite material at the time.

Hampstead Garden Suburb. The church of St Jude of 1909–11 offered a rare opportunity for Lutyens to fulfil his desire to build a church. The design was notionally Gothic to satisfy his forceful client Dame Henrietta Barnett, but Lutyens defiantly and successfully created a personal eclectic style. The intended pure-white interior was later decorated with First World War memorial murals.

create an ideal community that mixed the classes. The result was not quite as she had intended: shops were not built and the area became an entirely middle-class enclave – though it was famous internationally as a model of planned development. The layout, by Raymond Unwin, provided a large formal central green space in which were widely disposed a cultural institute and two churches – one Anglican and the other Free, each with a parsonage. For all these, as well as houses in North Square and Erskine Hill, Ned was appointed Consulting Architect and Designer. The silhouette of St Jude-on-the-Hill of 1909–11 is notionally Gothic to suit Henrietta Barnett, with whom he was not in tune, but Ned called it 'Romantic-Byzantine-cum-Nedi' and his eclecticism is highly successful, despite the jarring note of the Wealden trusses in the aisles. Its wonderful acoustics still attract sound

The cultural institute in Hampstead Garden Suburb was conceived in 1906–8 by Lutyens but completed by others.

26

The Free Church in Hampstead Garden Suburb was begun in 1911 by Lutyens but was not completed until much later by others.

recordists. Ned's intended pure-white interiors were not to be. The vicar met the war artist Walter Starmer in 1918 and commissioned the extensive murals that movingly adorn the church. Although not much given to such decoration, apart from that by his artist friend William Nicholson, Ned approved. While some of the building of the suburb was not completed until later by other architects, Ned's stamp was firmly in place.

Ned moved his office in 1910 from his family home to 17 Queen Anne's Gate in Westminster, a fairly rare example in London of houses of that queen's short reign. It was familiar ground, for Ned had already executed alterations at several houses nearby, including Edward Hudson's, outside which is a statue of the queen. Despite the economic consequences for the well-off of falling prices on the Stock Exchange and Lloyd George's 'People's Budget', and although some projects were cancelled, as always the rich have resources and Julius Drewe

15 and 17 Queen Anne's Gate, Westminster. In this outstanding enclave of Queen Anne houses built 1704–5, Lutyens remodelled number 15 in 1908 for Edward Hudson (with the statue of the queen on its flank wall) and had his offices at number 17 (1910– 31). He restored number 28 for the Liberal politician Lord Haldane and number 32 for Lady Allendale.

now came into Ned's life. Having made a fortune with the Home and Colonial Stores and retired at the age of thirty-three, Drewe wished to build a castle on a dramatic site on the edge of Dartmoor at Drewsteignton, which he believed to be the lair of his supposed Norman ancestor. This exciting project had a huge budget of £50,000, plus £10,000 for the garden, but Drewe remained vague about his needs. As the scheme for Castle Drogo developed and costs mounted with Drewe's desire for authentic 6 foot (1.8 metre) deep granite walls, it was scaled back substantially. Twenty years in the building and much truncated, this sharply profiled abstract-Tudor *folie de grandeur* remains brave and impressive, the last 'castle' in Britain, completed in 1930, a year before Drewe's death.

By contrast, Ned built one of his most charming 'Queen Anne' houses, The Salutation, Sandwich, Kent, for the banker Gaspard Farrer, one

Castle Drogo, Drewsteignton, Devon. The last 'castle' in England, on a dramatic site on the edge of Dartmoor. After twenty years in the building for Julius Drewe, a rich grocer, it was completed in 1930, a year before his death.

of three bachelor brothers, for whom Ned also built a neo-Georgian townhouse at 7 St James's Square, London. For another brother, Henry, a solicitor, he restored an office building in Lincoln's Inn Fields. At Great Dixter in East Sussex Ned sensitively restored and adapted with imported old materials a Tudor house for Nathaniel Lloyd, a retired printer who later wrote *A History of English Brickwork* and *History of the English House*, thanks to the interest kindled by Ned. However, not much save a ballroom came from the overtures of the tricky, penny-pinching Sir George Sitwell at Renishaw, Derbyshire. But there was work enough; by the end of 1910 there were sixty jobs listed, including the attractive Whalton Manor in Northumberland for the widowed Mrs Eustace Smith: a remodelling of houses on a village street into something grander.

Eve of the cataclysm

Overworked, Ned had to contend with a new threat to the uneasy tenor of his married life. Madame Mallet at Varengeville had embraced a strange new faith, Theosophy, which she introduced to Emily on her visit there in the spring of 1910. Enthralled, Emily enrolled in the Theosophical Society, directed by the manipulative Annie Besant. The weird ramifications of Theosophy are rather complicated but, in essence, its teachings led to Emily's vegetarianism and to the end of the couple's never-satisfactory sexual relations, and its mysticism provided such a strong focus of interest for Emily that, added to her obsessive interest in the creed's young Indian guru, Jiddu Krishnamurti, a heavy strain was put on their marriage. For Ned the only benefits were that Emily now had something to occupy herself with and that it led to a commission to build the society's headquarters in Bloomsbury (subsequently extended by others in Woburn Place as the British Medical Association). Some

compensation for the discord in their marriage was the job for the Mallets of building a *trianon* at Varengeville – Les Communes. It was lent to Emily for family holidays with Krishnamurti in tow, and so, with her deeply in thrall to Theosophy, the Lutyenses' marriage was no longer conjugal bliss, despite the evidence of their affectionate letters.

The steady stream of work continued, including a neo-Georgian house in Smith Square, Westminster, for Reginald McKenna, first Lord of the Admiralty, who married

36 Smith Square, Westminster. A neo-Georgian house built in 1911 for Reginald McKenna, then first Lord of the Admiralty, for whose family Lutyens built similar houses nearby.

The Theosophical Society Headquarters, Bloomsbury, London. The Burton Street elevation of 1911–13, built for the Society with which Lutyens's wife was closely involved, is a handsome brick palazzo. War intervened and the building was later taken over by the British Medical Association.

Herbert Jekyll's daughter Pamela, and other neo-Georgian houses were built nearby for Pamela's sister, Barbara McLaren, and her sister-in-law Lady Norman. McKenna became an important source of work for Ned from the 1920s. Now came work abroad. Partly thanks to the selfless support of Herbert Baker, already a well-established architect in South Africa, Ned was given, after initial local opposition, the Rand Regiment memorial and, via the forceful Mrs Lionel Phillips, the Johannesburg Art Gallery, the latter completed after his death.

With Britain's participation in three International Exhibitions – Brussels (1910), and Turin and Rome (1911) to celebrate Italy's fiftieth anniversary – Ned became further involved in public work, being appointed Consulting Architect to the Commission, of which his brother-in-law Lord Lytton was Chairman. At home there were problems with Emily's suffragette sister Constance, who had been arrested. Ned, rather apolitical and always disliking confrontation, fled to Rome with Lytton and his wife Pamela, pregnant by another man. Their quarrels, an attack of piles and the air of decay in the Eternal City made the trip a disappointment for Ned despite the opportunity to see for the first time buildings that were a source of his inspiration, but it resulted in his being given the job of designing the British Pavilion, based on Wren's St Paul's, which in turn led to its recreation as the British School in Rome.

31

An imperial palace and First World War commemoration

George V, the new king and emperor, proclaimed in December 1911 the transfer of the capital of the British Empire in India from Calcutta to Delhi – ostensibly for its central location and other supposedly pragmatic reasons but notably for political expediency in the fractious subcontinent. The long story of delays, bureaucracy, quarrels and jealousies engendered by the building of New Delhi until its inauguration in 1931 needs a book to itself. Opposed by the influential Lord Curzon on grounds of cost and by the Indians because its extreme climate made Delhi unsuitable as an all-year-round capital and Calcutta resented losing its status, the will of the viceroy, Lord Hardinge of Penshurst, prevailed and Ned was invited to join the Commission.

Apart from Ned's major work to honour the dead in the aftermath of the First World War, Delhi was his crowning achievement. Its centrepiece was the Viceroy's House, a great palace covering $4^{1}/_{2}$ acres (1.8 hectares) in a unique modern classicism invented by Ned and incorporating without pastiche a sense of Indian architecture, which he did not actually much admire. Appointed architect in 1913 on the recommendation of Reginald

Right: A drawing taken from a cartoon bust of 'Lut' made in 1917 by his staff at the Delhi office. This affectionate portrait, created from part of an architectural model of the dome of the Viceroy's House, was placed by Lutyens over the front door of his house in Mansfield Street.

The All-India War Memorial Arch, built 1921–31 at New Delhi, inspired by the Arc de Triomphe in Paris.

Blomfield, President of the Royal Institute of British Architects, Ned invited his old friend Herbert Baker to build the Secretariat, which he accepted despite some misgivings. They became co-architects but various issues, including the division of expenses, led to quarrels. The most serious matter was Ned's mistake in not realising that his triumphal way would have an uneven gradient that prevented an unobstructed vista of the Viceroy's House. This issue, which Ned called his 'Bakerloo', was, despite his endless petitioning, never resolved and rankled until his death.

The First World War, declared on 4th August 1914, marked a watershed in European civilisation; the confident Edwardian age was over. Work on New Delhi was cut back, the office staff was eventually reduced to two and some clients found it difficult to pay fees because of the fall in the stock market. The move to Bedford Square, a cold, damp house, was not a success and Ned's father died in 1915. With the overall gloom of the war and a strained marriage, Ned felt lonely during his trips to India. A new commission to build a palace in Spain for the Duke of Peñeranda lightened his mood, as did his election in 1916 to the Garrick Club. And for the first time the whole family enjoyed a summer holiday together in a Lutyens house – Folly Farm, lent, complete with servants, by Mrs Merton. Another significant event was Ned's meeting with the forceful, unhappily married Lady Sackville (mother of Vita Sackville-West), eight years older than himself, who introduced him to her society circle, including the Astors and Lady Diana Manners. Lady Sackville became a quarrelsome but initially generous client (she bought Ned a Rolls-Royce) and was almost certainly his only lover.

In 1917 General Fabian Ware, director of the newly constituted War Graves Commission, invited Ned and Baker to go to France and report on the military cemeteries and consider the monuments that should be erected. Greatly moved by the experience, Ned turned his energies to the creation of symbolic architecture of the highest order. His Cenotaph in Whitehall was initially conceived at Lloyd George's request as a saluting point for the march past of allied troops in July 1919. Rejecting any celebration of victory with heavy symbolism or glorification with cannons, Ned created a non-denominational memorial whose subtle and abstract design became the model for his subsequent war memorials. Its genius lies in its complicated geometry – the vertical, inclined planes meet at a point 1000 feet (304.8 metres) above ground while the horizontals are imperceptibly the circumference of a circle whose centre point is 900 feet (274.3 metres) below ground, a design requiring an immense number of calculations. The Cenotaph struck a chord with the general public, whose enthusiasm made his name widely known, but, shockingly, Ned was not invited to the unveiling ceremony.

The principal architects of the Imperial (now Commonwealth) War Graves Commission, Lutyens, Baker, Blomfield and later Charles Holden, built with their assistant architects nearly a thousand cemeteries in the north of France – 'The Silent Cities', as Rudyard Kipling called them – some immense, some tiny, in which lay over a million British and Commonwealth soldiers, mostly buried near where they fell. Ned's 8 ton monolithic Great War Stone, a sort of interdenominational altar bearing the inscription 'Their name liveth for evermore' (chosen by Kipling from *Ecclesiasticus*), and Blomfield's Cross of Sacrifice were

The Thiepval Memorial.

The unveiling of the Thiepval Memorial by the Prince of Wales on 16th May 1932 with Sir Fabian Ware at his side and Lutyens in the background (left).

placed in the larger cemeteries, which were usually graced by classical entrance lodges. Great care was taken with the landscaping of all cemeteries; even the smallest had beautifully planted gardens – leafy havens of eternal peace to honour the Fallen. An important feature of the graves was that there was no distinction between officers and men; all the white limestone headstones were of the same form, inscribed with name, rank and regimental badge, with a cross for Christians, the Star of David for Jews, and so on. Over the next twenty years, to commemorate the missing, many memorials were built, the finest of which by Lutyens in France were at Thiepval, Arras, Étaples, and at Villers-Bretonneux for the Australians. On a crest in Picardy, Thiepval, the Memorial to the Missing – a tall tower of tremendous power, brooding over the killing fields of the bloodiest conflict in British military history – is a complex stepped pyramidal brick structure with stone dressings consisting of a great arch with intersecting smaller arches, resulting in sixteen broad piers on which are inscribed the 73,357 names of those who fell in the Battle of the Somme and have no grave. With these memorials Ned created a sense of poignant, eternal reverence

Villers-Bretonneux, northern France. The view from Lutyens's Australian memorial of the wide landscape of the Somme, a scene of fierce fighting in the First World War. The memorial was inaugurated in 1938, little more than a year before the Second World War began.

for the multitude of soldiers who sacrificed their lives.

In Artois, on the edge of the city of Arras, Ned mastered an awkward site by creating a serene classical cloister, largely turning its back to a busy thoroughfare – the Royal Flying Corps Memorial, within which is a pylon with a winged globe carved by William Reid Dick. At the hospital cemetery at Étaples Ned built two tall matching arched cenotaphs, one at each end of a vast terrace looking out to the sea

The unveiling of the Faubourg d'Amiens British Military Cemetery at Arras on 31st July 1932 by Lord Trenchard. Lutyens stands in the centre, holding his top-hat. The man at the left of the picture, also with a top-hat, is believed to be Sir William Reid Dick, sculptor of the Royal Flying Corps Memorial, which stands in the cemetery cloister designed by Lutyens.

36

The Royal Flying Corps Memorial, Arras.

across the cemetery of more than ten thousand graves. Each cenotaph has four flags carved in stone, forever furled, a motif that Ned wanted but was not allowed to use for the Cenotaph in Whitehall. This abstract, non-denominational memorial set the pattern for his sublime memorials and cemeteries that rank among the most important and moving works of his whole career. Many other public and private war memorials were erected to Ned's designs in England, Ireland, India, Ceylon (Sri Lanka), New Zealand and South Africa. His reward, though ostensibly for New Delhi, was a knighthood in 1918. That year the family moved to 13 Mansfield Street, a large Adam house that proved as unwieldy as their previous houses but it was Ned's home until his death.

Étaples Military Cemetery, northern France – the prime example of Lutyens's major military cemeteries. The siting of the great twin pylons, one at each end of a broad terrace overlooking the many graves on a slope down to the sea, makes a powerful impression.

After the First World War, official recognition and a cathedral

Commissions for country houses were sparse after the war but in 1921 Ned built a large, dignified classical mansion in Lancashire – Gledstone Hall, for Sir Amos Nelson, a rich cotton merchant. That year he received the Gold Medal of the Royal Institute of British Architects, a distinction that moved him to tears, and the previous year he was elected Royal Academician. Much important work came from Reginald McKenna, now chairman of the Midland Bank, including the charming little Piccadilly branch, which pays homage to Wren's adjoining church of St James's, and the magnificent Italianate head office of 1924, which dominates the Poultry in the City of London. Other commercial schemes came his way later, including Reuter's in Fleet Street – another building juxtaposed with a Wren church, St Bride's, but this time a virtual skyscraper for its day. By contrast Queen Mary's Dolls' House, intended as a tribute to her inspiring role during the war, much engrossed Ned,

The former Midland Bank, Piccadilly, London, is an enchanting small building by Lutyens of 1922–4 that pays homage to his hero Wren, whose church of St James adjoins it.

Midland Bank Headquarters, Poultry, London, was built in 1924–39 on a grand Italianate scale with an immense banking hall. Lutyens owed the job to his friend Reginald McKenna, the bank's chairman.

Reuter's, Fleet Street, London. Lutyens's last commercial building of 1934–8 was a virtual skyscraper for its day with detail that excited American post-war post-modernist architects.

39

being a retreat from the tribulations of the real world, but at quite some cost to his own pocket. Conceived as an ideal gentleman's residence, this miniature palace in Ned's 'Wrenaissance' style was created at great expense with exquisite interiors by 250 artists and craftsmen. It proved very popular with the public when exhibited at the British Empire Exhibition at Wembley.

Apart from New Delhi, Ned's most important work was Britannic House in Finsbury Circus. The new headquarters for the Anglo-Persian Oil Company (later British Petroleum), this was a Baroque palace with a curved façade constructed at great expense and actually steel-framed behind its stone façade. It was some recompense for the bitter blow of losing to Herbert Baker the major commission to rebuild Soane's Bank of England. Ned did, however, build two grand classical pavilions and landscaped the setting of Soane's Tyringham Park in Buckinghamshire for F. A. König, a rich Theosophist.

In 1925, now Vice-President of the Royal Institute of British Architects, Ned went to New York to receive the Gold Medal from the Institute of American Architects and to discuss a new British Embassy in

Washington. He returned to his romantic roots in 1928 with the restoration of and extensions to Plumpton Place, an enchanted waterside retreat in Sussex for his old patron Edward Hudson. In the summer of 1929, from a chance meeting at Ned's favourite haunt, the Garrick Club, Dr Richard Downey, the Catholic Archbishop of Liverpool, asked Ned to discuss a new cathedral for

Britannic House, Finsbury Circus, London. Lutyens's commercial masterpiece, built in 1921–5 for the Anglo-Persian Oil Company, is as lavishly appointed as a palace, with marble floors and a grand staircase. The external figures are by the sculptor Derwent Wood and there is much carved detail by Broadbent.

The Mercantile Marine Memorial, Tower Hill, London, built in 1926–8. Lutyens's dignified classicism honours the men of the Merchant Navy and fishing fleets 'who have no known grave but the sea'.

The former YWCA, Great Russell Street, London – a chaste neo-Georgian composition of 1928 with good wrought ironwork.

The Great Model of Liverpool Roman Catholic Cathedral. The Second World War put paid to this ambitious project, of which only the crypt was built. The Great Model, 17 feet (5.2 metres) long, which took craftsmen two years to build at a cost of £5000, created a sensation when it was exhibited at the Royal Academy Summer Exhibition in 1934. The sculpture over the west entrance is by Charles Sergeant Jagger.

the city. Downey's ambition was to build the greatest in Christendom, with the largest dome in the world. Two months later Ned was off to India for the official opening of Viceroy's House and there learned that the king had conferred on him the KCIE (Knight Commander of the Order of the Indian Empire). During 1930 Ned was preoccupied with designing a Roman Catholic Cathedral for Liverpool. In June 1933 its foundation stone was laid and the crypt begun, not to be completed until 1941. This is all that was built of the cathedral; what would have been Ned's greatest work was abandoned and only the Great Model bears witness to its astonishing design. A new cathedral by Frederick Gibberd was built in 1959 over the crypt.

The last years

The 1930s, the autumn of Ned's life, was the decade in which he designed memorials for many of his friends and contemporaries, notably Gertrude Jekyll, who died in 1932, and Dame Nellie Melba. The fountains in Trafalgar Square of 1937–9 were in memory of two admirals, Lord Beatty and Lord Jellicoe, naval heroes and rivals. For the late King George V Ned designed a memorial at Windsor and, with the sculptor Reid Dick, the king's tomb in

Right: *The Northcliffe Memorial built by Lutyens in 1930 at St Dunstan-in-the-West, Fleet Street, to commemorate the newspaper magnate Viscount Northcliffe, founder of 'The Daily Mail'. The bust is by sculptor Kathleen Scott, widow of Scott of the Antarctic.*

Below: *The Trafalgar Square fountains were built by Lutyens in 1937–9 to commemorate two rival admirals, Jellicoe and Beatty. Bronze mermaids and mermen were added after the war by sculptors William McMillan and Sir Charles Wheeler.*

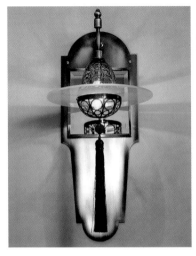

The 'Cardinal Hat' wall sconce, one of Lutyens's many witty designs for light fittings, was created for Campion Hall, the Jesuit foundation at Oxford that he designed in 1934.

St George's Chapel. His election in 1933 as Master of the Art Workers' Guild in Bloomsbury maintained his links with the Arts and Crafts movement. Nearby, in Great Russell Street, is his handsome neo-Georgian building for the Young Women's Christian Association. An unusual work in this period was the working-class housing scheme in Page Street, Westminster, for the City Council; this comprises a series of blocks of flats with rather startling chequer-board-patterned façades built around courtyards, with the entrance pavilions serving as shops. In Oxford he built Campion Hall for the Jesuits, but in London his scheme for a National Theatre opposite the Victoria and Albert Museum was not adopted, nor was its successor on the South Bank. In 1938, the year he became President of the Royal Academy, Ned made the last of his nineteen trips to India, this time to remove tasteless alterations to his masterpiece effected by the vicereine, Lady Willingdon.

Ned designed Middleton Park in Oxfordshire for the Earl of Jersey in collaboration with his son Robert, with whom he was reconciled

Page Street housing, Westminster. This unusually interesting council housing scheme built in 1929–35 by Lutyens blends modernist planning, enlivened by elaborate chequer-board patterning, with classical pavilions serving as shops.

Compton, Surrey. The Guildford bypass bridge crossing the alleged route of the Pilgrims' Way was built in 1939 by Lutyens in his characteristic small mellow hand-made brick with his Cross of Sacrifice, which features in some First World War cemeteries.

after years of estrangement. The second Lady Jersey, an American film star briefly married previously to Cary Grant, had expensive tastes and required fourteen bathrooms. An E-shaped Georgian house with shutters giving it a French feel and with four distinctive entrance lodges, Middleton Park was Ned's last country house. Completed in 1938, just before the outbreak of war, it was little used and was later converted into flats.

Ned remained in London during the war, weakened after a bout of pneumonia and a thrombosis. He continued to work on Liverpool Cathedral, and a plan for the post-war reconstruction of London kept his mind active. In 1942 he received the Order of Merit; he was the first architect to receive this honour. A pipe smoker all his life, Ned died of lung cancer in his seventy-fifth year, early on New Year's Day in 1944. A grand funeral took place in Westminster Abbey. His ashes, contained in an urn designed by his son, were placed in the crypt of St Paul's Cathedral. Emily lived on until 1964. As for their children, Barbara (1898–1981) married Euan Wallace; he died of cancer, three of his sons were killed in the Second World War and a fourth son died during an operation. Barbara married a second time but committed suicide after the death of her surviving son by Euan. Robert (1901–72) had quite a successful architectural practice; he married three times, and his schizophrenic son by his first wife died in 1929. His daughter Candia produces Lutyens furniture designs to order. Ursula (1904–67) married Viscount Ridley, had two children and adopted a third but committed suicide. Elizabeth (1906–83) never married but became a well-known composer. Mary (1908–99) became happy with her second marriage, to J. G. Links, and produced several biographies, including an excellent memoir of her father.

Further reading

Amery, Colin, and Richardson, Margaret (editors). *Catalogue of the Lutyens Exhibition*. Arts Council of Great Britain, 1981.

Audoin-Rouzeau, Stéphane, and Becker, Annette. *1914–1918: Understanding the Great War*. Profile Books, 2002.

Barker, Michael, and Atterbury, Paul. *The North of France*. Heyford Press, 1990. Includes a section on the Somme.

Brown, Jane. *Lutyens and the Edwardians*. Viking, 1996. Provides a detailed list of buildings to see.

Gradidge, Roderick. *Edwin Lutyens: Architect Laureate*. Allen & Unwin, 1981.

Hopkins, Andrew, and Stamp, Gavin (editors). *Lutyens Abroad*. British School at Rome, 2002.

Hussey, Christopher. *Life of Lutyens*. Country Life, 1950.

Inskip, Peter. *Edwin Lutyens*. Academy, 1979.

Longworth, Philip. *The Unending Vigil*. Leo Cooper and Secker & Warburg, 1985.

Lutyens, Mary. *Edwin Lutyens: A Memoir*. John Murray, 1980.

Nath, Aman. *Dome over India*. India Book House Pvt Ltd, 2000. A lavishly illustrated account of New Delhi.

Percy, Clayre, and Ridley, Jane (editors). *The Letters of Edwin Lutyens*. Collins, 1985.

Richardson, Margaret. *Catalogue of the Drawings Collection of the RIBA: Lutyens*. Gregg, 1973.

Richardson, Margaret. *Sketches by Edwin Lutyens*. Academy, 1994.

Ridley, Jane. *The Architect and His Wife: A Life of Edwin Lutyens*. Chatto & Windus, 2002.

Stamp, Gavin. *Silent Cities*. RIBA, 1977.

Stamp, Gavin. *Edwin Lutyens: Country Houses*. Aurum Press, 2001.

Wilhide, Elizabeth. *Sir Edwin Lutyens*. Pavilion, 2000.

The Buildings of England, Scotland and *Wales* series (Penguin and Yale University Press), originally by Nikolaus Pevsner but since revised by various authors, has volumes covering each county of England, Wales and Scotland, with several for London. The books provide the most complete coverage of the architecture of Great Britain and contain descriptions of the majority of Lutyens's buildings.

Lutyens sitting in his favourite chair, called the 'Napoleon'. This chair is his own design but is based on one used by the French emperor, apparently noticed by Lutyens in a painting.

Places to visit

Lutyens's buildings in London can be viewed from the street and his churches at Hampstead Garden Suburb may be visited. The war cemeteries and monuments in the north of France are all accessible and at Thiepval a Visitor Centre (telephone: 00 33 322 74 60 47) displaying Lutyens's works was inaugurated in 2004 by the Duke of Kent. Few of his country houses are open to the public but the following may be visited during the summer months: Castle Drogo (Drewsteignton, Devon EX6 6PB; telephone 01647 433306); Lindisfarne Castle (Holy Island, Berwick-upon-Tweed, Northumberland TD15 2SH; telephone 01289 389244) (both National Trust properties – website: www.nationaltrust.org.uk); Goddards (Abinger Common, Dorking, Surrey RH5 6JH; Landmark Trust, telephone: 01306 730871; website: www.landmarktrust.org.uk); Knebworth House (Knebworth, Stevenage, Hertfordshire SG3 6PY; telephone 01438 812661; website: www.knebworthhouse.com); Le Bois des Moutiers (Varengeville, Normandy). Little Thakeham (Storrington, Sussex) is run as a hotel, as is Grey Walls (Gullane, near Edinburgh). Queen Mary's Dolls' House is on permanent display at Windsor Castle (Windsor, Berkshire SL4 2AP; telephone 020 7766 7304; website: www.royal.gov.uk). The Great Model of Liverpool Cathedral is at the city's Walker Art Gallery (William Brown Street, Liverpool L3 8EL; telephone 0151 478 4199; website: www.liverpoolmuseums.org.uk). A number of gardens are open under the National Gardens Scheme.

The Lutyens Trust (Goddards, Abinger Common, Dorking, Surrey RH5 6JH; telephone: 01306 730487; website: www.lutyenstrust.org.uk) is devoted to conserving Lutyens's buildings and protecting the spirit of his works.

Lutyens Design Associates (3 Egerton Terrace, London SW3 2BX; telephone 020 7589 2347; website: www.lutyens-furniture.com), was founded by his grand-daughter and produces Lutyens furniture and lighting to order from his original drawings.

The Royal Naval Division Memorial in Horse Guards Parade, Westminster. Dedicated in 1925, it was removed in 1940 for safety and then re-erected at the Royal Naval College, Greenwich, until that closed as a naval establishment. The memorial was returned to its original site in 2003.

Index